FRUCTOSE

SALICYLATES POLYOLS

MALABSORPTION

AMINES FRUCTANS

WHAT'S

FRUCTOSE GLUTAMATES

IN

GALACTANS OXALATES

WHAT

JOAN MAGUIRE

Copyright Page

New: Fructose Malabsorption What's In What

Author: Joan Maguire

National Library of Australia Cataloguing-in-Publication – Publication entry

A catalogue record for this book is available from the National Library of Australia

Published with the assistance of CreateSpace and Draft2Digital is available through www.helpfuldietaryrecipes.com

This book was created and written By Joan Maguire on18th July 2017©
ISBN: 9780994543196

E-book written August 2017© and is available through the providers on www.helpfuldietaryrecipes.com
EISBN: 9780648220602

Large Print version created on 7th February 2018©
ISBN: 9780648220626 (large print)

DEDICATION

I would like to dedicate this book and say
to thank you to my Earth Angel David
and his friends, who inspire and motivate
me to achieve things that I never dreamt,
were possible.

You have been my saviours many times
when I have wanted to give up on life

And to all the people who in one way or
another have to cope each day with food
intolerances that have been discovered
and known about for many years and
those medical conditions that have just
been discovered in recent years.

INTRODUCTION

I usually start my books by thanking the many people who have so frustratingly spent many hours on the research that I am about to share with you. Some of this information goes back to 2013 when I was first diagnosed with Fructose Malabsorption and sadly some of the sites are no longer there on the internet.

They say that Fructose Malabsorption is a complicated medical condition, and it is. There are so many pieces to it that are only being discovered now and most times there are other medical conditions that people like me have to deal with as well.

In this book I will give you the information that I have gathered for myself from many, many internet sites and it's a pity that a few of the really good ones are not on the net anymore.

I will try to explain the different parts of Fructose Malabsorption, or as I sometimes call it FM, and some of the other medical conditions that can also be attached.

I am not qualified in anything so please don't think that I have every answer and that all the information is the gospel truth; in fact, a lot of the information on the different web sites can be very conflicting and only give the information that is required by their site.

The information in this book pertains to what is in different foods that we all eat most of the time. I have not included any type of alcohol as it is made with different ingredients and in different ways all over the world. Soft drinks are the same.

I was not able to list every food as there wasn't information on a lot of it; however, I have done my best to include as many as I could from my lists of the last five years.

Through listening to different people, I have found out that Amines and

Glutamates are also other issues that affect people with Fructose Malabsorption; so I am including these issues into this book.

ACKNOWLEDGEMENTS

I would like to thank my immediate family for their positive support when times for me were tough, even though they didn't know what I was going through at times.

I would like to thank the many, many people on the numerous web sites that have given me most of the information that I required at the time and still use often. I am not able to even name you all without writing another book.

I would like to thank the few close friends who have just sat and listened to me when I needed to talk; again they didn't really know what I was going through at the time.

I would also like to thank everyone else who has helped me bring this book to life and to you. I hope that it will be a learning experience for you as it has been for me and that you may be able to help yourself or someone else with some of the information that this book contains.

I would like to thank all the other people, who shall remain nameless, you know who you are, for being there for me and going through the good and bad times that I have had without judgement.

OTHER BOOKS IN THE COOKBOOK SERIES

Helpful Dietary Recipes For Most
Intolerance

Helpful Dietary Recipes For Most
Intolerance
International Cuisine

Helpful Dietary Recipes For Most
Intolerance
Condiments

Fructose Malabsorption Dealing With It
My Way

This book and the other books are
available as eBooks and through
www.helpfuldietaryrecipes.com and
Amazon

CONTENTS

THE EARLY YEARS

In the introduction I stated that Fructose Malabsorption (FM) is a complicated medical condition. Most people would know of Irritable Bowel Syndrome which is one of the earlier diagnoses for FM. There is a lot that I can say but I'm not going to as you will get the main gist from the story without a lot of repeats.

Legally, I have to say why I wrote my cookbooks and now writing the second of the books that explains in more detail about Fructose Malabsorption. This time it will be a shorter explanation.

I was diagnosed with Irritable Bowel Syndrome way back in 1971 and was told then that it was brought on by stress and there was nothing that could be done for it.

My mother had told me that I was a very "windy" baby and she used to give me orange juice to help with my constipation, but it never did anything but make me worse.

This may have been the beginning of my issue and nobody knew of FM back in 1951 in England.

Dad had an allotment where he grew some of our vegetables, so we were all raised on a healthy diet. Mum also baked healthy snacks and cakes for us.

In 1957 our family came to Australia and we settled in Adelaide, South Australia where my father's parents and brothers lived. I don't really remember that much because I was still rather young but many photos from those years showed that I had a bit of a "pot belly" but none of my brothers or sisters had one.

I used to be known as "Fatty Patty" because my middle name is Patricia or Joanie and I used to become angry over it, so much that I used to hate my middle name and sometimes shorten my first name to Jo.

I used to always keep to myself because of it. Other girls my age wouldn't have much to do with me because I was "too fat" to fit in with their groups.

I was tested for Myopia (short sightedness) at the age of nine and had to wear glasses and these also were another form of name calling for me and another reason why I was not accepted by the other girls. I was "short and dorky", not tall and slim like them.

When I got married, I bought a beautiful wedding dress but as the wedding drew nearer; my mother had to alter it because I began bloating more often, I kept getting bigger. Mind you, it would come and go and on my wedding day, my stomach had bloated in a way that I looked like I was in the early stages of pregnancy but my mother was able to fix my dress to hide it. I know she wasn't happy about the way I looked but she never said anything that day.

Not long after I was married, I fell pregnant with my beautiful eldest daughter, so I had an excuse for being "fat". This time people used to say that if I fell over, I would just lay there and rock back and forth. Another comment that hurt; however, I never showed my feelings because it always led to more nasty comments.

Two years after my first daughter was born, we found out that she had a serious medical condition and would need surgery. I was pregnant with my amazing second daughter and this news didn't help my medical condition at all.

With a new baby, a daughter who had just had major surgery I became most unwell and went to my doctor who informed me that I had Irritable Bowel Syndrome brought on by the stress I was going through and there wasn't anything they or I could do about it except to stop stressing.

They also stated that I had a mental health issue (anxiety) and put me on anti-depression drugs.

Our diet had always been good and there was little that I had to do to change my eldest daughter's diet after her operation.

Two years later my wonderful son was born and a few years later things started to go wrong in my marriage. My husband found someone younger and slimmer than me and left to live with her, leaving me to raise my children. He would come back and we would move to another state to start a new life.

I will only say that this went on for thirty years but my self-confidence was gone, I hated myself completely and my so called IBS got worse. I only wore clothes that were size 20 or bigger.

Now, I stated earlier that I was short; I am 152cm tall or just a fraction over 5 feet so being the size I was didn't look good at all.

I was accused of being obese, lazy and a hypochondriac but I wasn't any of them.

I would go to the doctors often because of my bloating issue and all they wanted to do was to give me more drugs and suggested that I should find a counsellor.

My children had grown and left home and I got a divorce and sought help wherever I could find it. I also took up dancing 50s & 60s rock and roll and I enjoyed it very much. It was a good form of exercise for me and a very good stress release. I had a dance partner but that was it; the past reared its ugly head again; I was good to dance with but the so called "package" was not good enough to be seen out with. I was too short and too fat. Bloated meant fat.

I decided to go back to study and get myself a career so I enrolled in a TAFE course to do Community Service.

Two years later, I left with four diplomas and three certificate fours in several branches of Community Service and Community Housing.

During two of my diploma courses I learnt about what drugs can do to your mental health and how to control and keep most mental health issue at bay. I was also very fortunate to have a very good doctor who would work with me and we would often exchange information and learn from each other.

I went to see my doctor, who I will call Dr. J, one day and it just so happen to be a really bad day for me and the bloating. He couldn't believe that I could be so big that I had trouble breathing, let alone walking so he sent me for a blood test.

The results came back stating there was something wrong with my glucose so I had to have another test done where I had to blow up a helium balloon with a straw.

The results came back stating that I was a Type 2 Diabetic. (FM was not known of at that time and the tests are the same).

Dr. J knew that my diet was based around me cooking and eating fresh vegetables and I ate very little junk food. I never ate fruit, drank alcohol, fizzy drinks or fruit juice because of the wing/gas effect that they would have on me. I did enjoy my tea and coffee though.

I am also a smoker so I tried some of the quit smoking products. One worked for a little while. However, my bloating became so severe that Dr. J arranged for me to have an Endoscopy done to find out what was wrong.

Two years after I was diagnosed as a Type 2 Diabetic I went in to have my Endoscopy done. Before I was wheeled in to the theatre, the surgeon (Dr. M) came out and asked me some questions; like my name, age and why I was there.

When I told him about my bloating issue he stated that it sounded like I have FM and have most probably had it since I was a baby but not born with it.

He also stated that it had only been discovered about eight to ten years ago and there weren't that many doctors who knew about it and there was some information on it but not much. There weren't really any specific tests that can be done to prove it so it would be all trial and error on my part.

Was this the reason I had been suffering all my life?

The following day I started my research on FM and cut all the vegetables out of my diet. I was fine eating meat and dairy. Unfortunately I was no longer able to enjoy my cups of coffee during the day and my tea at night because they both had Polyols in them. If I drank any sort of tea at night I would be awake around four in the morning with pains in my stomach that were like being in labour with my three grown children at the same time. The pain would not go until I passed the wind/gas.

When my stomach is so bad, I can't do anything. I get frustrated, go into a downward slide quickly into depression and I just want to give up on life. It can take me anywhere between one week to a month to pull myself back into a sort of normal life.

I know that there are some people out there nodding their heads yes because they go through it as well. FM does control your life until you learn how to deal with it to suit your own needs. It does cause mental health issues due to the fact that eating out is very hard because you have to be very careful with what you put in your mouth and people won't invite you to join them because of it.

I went out to dinner with my daughters back in February 2017 and we went to a place where I knew I could eat certain foods like a chicken schnitzel; the only thing is, the place now adds onion powder to the breadcrumbs and that alone gave me issue starting twenty minutes after I had finished eating and for the following three weeks.

There wasn't anything mentioned even after I had spoken to them about my FM. They didn't really listen to me and I was thought of as being fussy and they thought that I wouldn't even notice.

Yes, I have been to and spoken to many dieticians and other nutritionists who all think they know best about your body and they don't appreciate you saying otherwise.

I do have to mention this so please don't get me wrong because this happened to me. I went to see the dietician at the same hospital where I had my Endoscopy and she and I had a few words concerning the FODMAP diet. I told her that I had tried it before several times and my body couldn't handle it.

I have never seen anyone go into a tantrum so quickly because she knew what was best for me so to stop the tantrum I said I would try it again. Thirteen days later I was back at my doctors with bloating, walking and breathing issues and he nearly had a fit when he saw me and I told him what had happened.

He gave me a good telling off and took me straight off the diet because it was killing me due to the wind/gas build up was squashing my lungs and my heart and sent me straight back to the dietician to let her see what she had done to me. The dieticians comment was "Well we had to try it didn't we". There wasn't any apology from her.

I have tried seeing other dieticians for help and one teaching place actually asked me not to come back because I was too complicated and they couldn't help me and didn't want to know.

I have found out that other family members have Fructose Malabsorption; however, it affects them differently to me.

This is a snippet that someone gave me and whether it is true, I can't really say.

"CAUSES OF FRUCTOSE INTOLERANCE"

Blame your parents! All food intolerance is genetic – so you got it from your parents and grandparents. A very small percentage of people have the more serious form of Fructose Intolerance (less than 1 in 10,000 people).

THE REASONS FM IS COMPLICATE

Don't forget that this is the research that I have found out to help me with my issue and it may not be correct and it may be conflicting to what you know. My main issue with FM is the Polyols; the sugar alcohols that not many health practioners from all areas know about or know little about.

I will also be putting in some information that I have taken from the net and if I can cite the web site then I will. Other information may be from my files or from web sites that are no longer available or just snippets from different web sites. Also the information may have come from one particular web site but it can also be found on other ones.

Please don't bite my head off if you think that I have used your information for my educational book and haven't acknowledged you but your site may not have been the one that I took it from.

All sites on these issues are helpful to me and other people; however, I may just be bringing it all together so I thank you for your long, hard and frustrating work.

Fructose Malabsorption is made up in a few parts. First there is Fructose which is the natural sugar in just about everything. Then there are Fructans which is mainly wheat products and is in some form in fruit and vegetables. Then there is the Polyols or sugar alcohol that is in everything. It is the natural sugar that God gave to each plant as a food source to help it grow. Then there is the Galactans which are also wind/gas causing parts in most foods.

A BRIEF SUMMARY ON FRUCTOSE MALABSORPTION

This information was taken from: http://www.marksdailyapple.com/fodmaps/#ixzz4Cqm7oyio
"You could be having a fairly routine conversation about health and nutrition where everything discussed is familiar.

You hear things like "carbs" and "medium chain triglycerides" and "fructose" and "macros" and "gluten" and "PUFAs," thinking nothing of it. Like I said, routine. Then someone mentions FODMAPs. Huh? What the heck is that?

Quite possibly one of the strangest, seemingly contrived acronyms in existence, FODMAPs represents a collection of foods to which a surprisingly large number of people are highly sensitive. To them, paying attention to the FODMAPs in their diets is very real and very serious if they hope to avoid debilitating, embarrassing, and painful digestive issues.

To begin, what exactly are FODMAPs?

As I said, it's an acronym:

F is for Fermentable – Fermentable carbohydrates are carbohydrates that are fermented by bacteria instead of broken down by our digestive enzymes. In most people, some fermentable carbohydrates are healthy sources of food for the (helpful) bacteria that ferment them; these can include the prebiotics I've championed in the past and can actually improve digestive and overall health. In people with FODMAPs intolerance, certain carbohydrates can become too fermentable, resulting in gas, bloating, pain, and poor digestion, as well as proliferation of unwanted pathogenic bacteria.

O is for Oligosaccharides – Oligosaccharides are short-chain carbohydrates, including fructans (fructooligosaccharides, or FOS, and inulin) and galactans (raffinose and stachyose). Fructans are chains of fructose with a glucose molecule at the end; galactans are chains of galactose with a fructose molecule.

D is for Disaccharides – These are pairs of sugar molecules, with the most problematic being the milk sugar lactose (a galactose molecule with a glucose molecule).

M is for Monosaccharides – This describes a single sugar molecule. Free fructose is the monosaccharide to watch out for with FODMAPs intolerance.

A is for And – Every list needs a good conjunction.

P is for Polyols – Polyols include sugar alcohols like xylitol, sorbitol, or maltitol. For an idea as to their effects, type one of them into Google and note the autofill choice (hint: it's usually "diarrhea" or "constipation" or "gas").

Since large amounts of polyols rarely occur in nature, lots of people have trouble with them.

The reality, of course, is that digestive difficulties are widespread, particularly in the industrialized world. If it's not constipation, it is diarrhea, or bloating, or gas, or hemorrhoids, or IBS, or all of the above. These complaints are sadly very common (even more common than the stats would suggest, since many people are too embarrassed to admit they have an issue).

For many of these people, FODMAPs may be exacerbating their symptoms.

Normal carbohydrate digestion takes place in the small intestine, where polysaccharides are broken up into glucose, fructose, and galactose and transporters like GLUT2 and GLUT5 absorb them for the body to use as nutrients. Sometimes those sugar molecules make it past the small intestine into the large intestine where colonic bacteria – the gut flora we (sorta) know and love – gobbles it up via fermentation, potentially causing gas and painful bloating.

The presence of too many sugars in the colon can also cause an influx of fluid, which could lead to diarrhea. Constipation is another common symptom, though it's not clear exactly how FODMAPs cause it. And some polysaccharides, like the oligosaccharides, make it through to the colonic bacteria as a rule because they resist digestion in everyone (in healthy people, these have a useful prebiotic effect).

You might be thinking, "Cool, so I can just avoid those weird sounding sugars and be fine, right?" Probably not. FODMAPs are very prevalent in the food supply. Even if you avoid free fructose, don't drink milk, and ditch processed food containing sugar alcohols, you'll still run into them in many fruits and vegetables.

FODMAP-containing vegetables include:

Asparagus (fructose, fructans), artichoke (fructose), beets (fructans), broccoli (fructans), Brussels sprouts (fructans), butternut squash (fructans), cabbage (fructans), celery (polyols), cauliflower (polyols), eggplant, fennel (fructans), garlic (fructans), leek (fructans), mushroom (polyols), okra (fructans), onion (fructans), shallots (fructans), sweet corn (fructose), radicchio (fructans), sweet potato (polyol)

FODMAP-containing fruits:

Apples (fructose, polyol), apricots (polyol), avocados (polyol), blackberries (polyol), cherries (fructose, polyol), plums (polyol), pluots (polyol), lychees (polyol), nectarines (polyol), peaches (polyol), pears (fructose, polyol), persimmons (polyol), grapes (fructose), mango (fructose), watermelon (polyol, fructose), dried fruit (fructose), juice (fructose)

Plus sweeteners like honey, agave nectar, maltitol, sorbitol, mannitol, and xylitol. And any dairy that contains significant amounts of lactose, like milk or soft cheeses. Depending on your sensitivity, cream or butter can even do the trick.

So it covers quite a few otherwise healthy Primal foods (and some non-Primal ones, like wheat and rye and the aforementioned refined sweeteners).

Let me reiterate before I go on, because I don't want to scare everyone away from berries and broccoli: not everyone has problems with FODMAPs.

Most people probably don't. If you're eating all that stuff without issue, continue doing so and consider this post merely an academic curiosity.

Who might benefit from limiting FODMAPs?

Anyone with small intestinal bacterial overgrowth (SIBO)

Normally, the small intestine has relatively low numbers of gut flora residents. In SIBO, it's got tons that aren't supposed to be there. They interfere with nutrient absorption, digestion, and just generally muck everything up. SIBO has been shown to correlate quite strongly with lactase deficiency. Without enough lactase, you won't be able to digest lactose (one of the premier FODMAPs) and your colonic bacteria will have to do the job. Another, earlier study found that patients with SIBO also show malabsorption of fructose and sorbitol in addition to lactose; all three are FODMAPs.

Anyone with IBS

Low-FODMAP diets beat the pants off conventional dietary advice for people with IBS. One study found that while healthy subjects had increased flatulence on a high-FODMAP diet, subjects with IBS had increased flatulence in addition to lethargy and adverse GI symptoms. This could indicate that both groups were feeding FODMAPs to their gut bugs (which produce the flatulence through fermentation), but only the IBS patients had enough pathogenic gut flora to produce adverse symptoms.

Anyone suffering from chronic stress

Stress is a well-known disruptor of digestive function as anyone who's gotten queasy, lost their appetite, or had explosive diarrhea before the big interview could tell you. There's evidence that stress might be causing FODMAP-intolerance, too. First, stress inhibits the action of GLUT2, a transporter responsible for the small intestinal absorption of glucose, fructose, and galactose in the gut. If you're unable to adequately absorb the sugar molecules in the small intestine, they end up making it to your large intestine for fermentation by colonic bacteria. Second, stress has an immediate impact on the composition and function of your gut flora, rendering your populations less diverse and allowing certain pathogenic species to overpopulate.

Anyone with otherwise unexplained digestive problems
Maybe you haven't had a diagnosis. Maybe you just don't feel right after eating almost anything. Maybe you're chronically constipated (or the opposite). Trying a low-FODMAP diet can help you narrow your focus and start to identify some culprits.

If you decide to embark on a low-FODMAP diet, consider keeping a diet journal to log your food and track your reactions to individual FODMAPs.

Some people might really react poorly to fructose while having no issues with lactose. Point being: different FODMAPs affect different people differently. You can tolerate some and not others.

Dosage matters, too. A gram of inulin might be fine, while five grams could cause distress.
Individual tolerance must be determined by, well, seeing what and how much you tolerate.

If you're interested in healing your gut, whether from SIBO or IBS or anything else that might be predisposing you to FODMAP intolerance, well-established protocol like GAPS (Gut and Psychology Syndrome) diet or SCD (specific carbohydrate diet) may help and are worth looking into.

If you have no digestive issues, I would caution against trying a low-FODMAP diet "just because". You'll be missing out on some very nutritious, important foods, probably unnecessarily, while adding a bunch of unnecessary stress to your eating. FODMAP-related digestive issues are very noticeable. You'll know it if you have it".

Some people can be born with Hereditary Fructose Malabsorption or get it when they are babies. The surgeon who did my Endoscopy thinks that's when I may have got it.

Another snippet about Fructose Malabsorption that we need to remember comes from http://www.strandsofmylife.com/8-symptoms-fodmap-intolerance-explained/

"All fruits and vegetables contain fructose and many contain fructans and polyols, which can cause us folk problems.

Some are lower in these substances than others and so can be tolerated in small helpings. Your digestive system rules your life.

Of course, this rules your life. I have always wondered what it would be like to not have to constantly think about this issue and how it would impact on each of my decisions in life. I know now because I have it under control – finally. I seldom worry about toilets any longer but must always be aware of what goes into my mouth. If I suffer or not is now up to me. Not to fate".

WHAT ARE FRUCTANS AND GALACTO-OLIGOSACCHARIDES?

This information was taken from: http://fodmapfriendly.com/what-are-fodmaps/what-are-fructans-and-galacto-oligosaccharides/

Fructans are fructose polymers and are the naturally occurring storage carbohydrates of a variety of vegetables, including onions and garlic, fruits and cereals.

Additional sources of fructans are inulin or Fructo-oligosaccharides (FOS). Inulin and FOS are increasingly being added to foods for their known prebiotic effects. The human small intestine does not produce enzymes capable of hydrolyzing these fructose-fructose bonds and as such fructans cannot be absorbed across the small intestine. They are then delivered into the large bowel, where they can be readily fermented by colonic bacteria. Fructans alone can induce abdominal symptoms and can also exaggerate those associated with fructose malabsorption or lactose intolerance.

Hence, fructans are often limited in any dietary modification for patients with fructose malabsorption and IBS.

Like fructans, galacto-oligosaccharides or chains of galactose molecules are also malabsorbed in the small intestine. Individuals do not produce enzymes that hydrolyze galactose-galactose bonds and they too are readily fermented by bacteria in the large bowel.

Significant dietary sources of galactans (raffinose and stacchyose) include legumes such as lentils, chickpeas and red kidney beans.

Vegetarians often consume large amounts of galactans due to increased consumption of legumes as they often provide an important source of protein in a vegetarian diet.

A little bit of information on Galactans: "Galactooligosaccharides (GOS) are short chains of galactose molecules that can cause symptoms due to fermentation. It should be noted that the GOS are generally found in legumes and seaweed and many foods have not been characterized regarding their GOS content".

Sugar Alcohols: Everything You Need to Know By Mark Sisson http://www.marksdailyapple.com/sugar-alcohols/

I've been on a bit of an alternative sweetener kick these past few weeks, for good reason: people want and need to know about this stuff. While a purist shudders at the prospect of any non- or hypo-caloric sugar substitute gracing his or her tongue, I'm a realist. People are going to partake and it's important to understand what's entering your body and what, if any, effects it will have.

Whether it's diet soda, artificial sweeteners, stevia, or the mysterious sugar alcohols, people want the sweet without worrying about a big physiological effect – an insulin surge, a blood glucose dip, even a migraine. So I've been covering the various types and have tried to be comprehensive about it. As a whole, it all seems fairly safe. Alternative sweeteners might mess with some folks' adherence to a low-sugar diet, and they might induce or fortify cravings, but the research doesn't suggest that they're going to give you cancer or diabetes. The potentially negative effects are all fairly subjective, so it's safe to play around with them and determine their role in your life based on how they affect your appetite, state-of-mind, and any other subjective health markers.

One remains, however. I have yet to cover sugar alcohols. I was surprised, actually, having gone through my archives and finding nothing. Sugar alcohols are pretty prominent in the low-carb world – all those sugar-free desserts and chocolates and protein bars geared toward Atkins types tend to use sugar alcohols – so I had better get to it, huh?

What Are Sugar Alcohols?
A sugar alcohol, also known as a polyol, is an interesting type of carbohydrate. Its structure is kind of a hybrid between a sugar molecule and an alcohol molecule (hence the name "sugar alcohol") and,

for the most part, our bodies do a poor job of digesting and breaking down sugar alcohol in the small bowel. It's also sweet to the tongue and resistant to fermentation by oral bacteria, meaning sugar-free gum manufacturers employ it judiciously to sweeten their products without causing cavities. Our colonic bacteria, however, can and do ferment the stuff. For that reason, it's a kind of prebiotic that, as Kurt Harris points out, can stimulate diarrhea and exacerbate existing irritable bowel syndrome-related symptoms. Common side effects of sugar alcohol consumption (or over-consumption) include bloating, gas, and abdominal pain.

Sugar alcohols are not quite non-caloric, but all contribute fewer calories than sucrose, and their effects on insulin and blood sugar (if any) are pretty minimal.

Sugar alcohols pop up in nature, in fruits like apples and pears, but any commercial product that contains them must list the specific alcohols in the ingredients. If they aren't counted toward the official carb count, they must be listed separately in the nutritional information. Let's look at some of the popular ones you'll be encountering:

Xylitol – Glycemic Index of 13
Xylitol is one of the more popular sugar alcohols. It tastes remarkably like sucrose, has about half the calories, and is 1.6 times as sweet, with little effect on blood glucose and none on insulin levels.

You can find xylitol in certain berries, corn husks, mushroom fibers, and oats; most commercial xylitol comes from hardwood and corn. Xylitol has a cooling effect on the mouth and is actively protective against dental caries (as opposed to merely being neutral or non-contributive, like the other sugar alcohols), making it the favorite choice of sugar-free chewing gum makers.

There appear to be some interesting health benefits to xylitol, too, beyond the well-established preventive actions against dental plaque and cavities. Xylitol shows promise as a bone remineralization agent, positively affecting both tooth enamel and bone mineral density (albeit, thus far, in rats). I count at least ten studies showing xylitol's promise in the treatment or prevention of osteoporosis. Just don't feed it to your dog. Also, it may exacerbate intestinal distress or cause diarrhea, so exercise caution (and linger near a toilet if you're unsure of its effect on you).

Sorbitol – Glycemic Index of 9

Sorbitol is found primarily in stone fruits, and manufacturers use it in diet sodas, sugar-free ice creams and desserts, as well as mints, cough syrups, and gum. It's about half as sweet as sucrose, with 2.6 calories per gram (compared to sucrose's 4 calories per gram, of course). Being a polyol, it has the potential to cause great gastrointestinal distress, especially in patients with IBS. This is compounded by its relative lack of sweetness when compared to other polyols, like xylitol; people are more likely to consume greater amounts of sorbitol to attain the desired level of sweetness and companies are more likely to use more of it.

There don't appear to be any proactive beneficial effects with sorbitol. It doesn't affect insulin or blood glucose, which could be good for diabetics, but there's nothing like xylitol's promise.

Erythritol – Glycemic Index of 0
Erythritol is almost non-caloric (0.2 calories per gram) and about 60-70% as sweet as sugar. It's the only sugar alcohol that doesn't appear to cause gastrointestinal distress (because the body absorbs it rather than let it pass to the colon for fermentation), it doesn't affect blood sugar or insulin, and it cannot be fermented by dental bacteria (and it exhibits some of xylitol's inhibitory effect on carie-causing oral bacteria, though not all of it).

For the most part, erythritol seems pretty safe, and it's rumored to taste very similar to sugar. Overconsumption – taking in more than your body can absorb – can result in bloating and gastrointestinal distress, but it takes a lot.

Maltitol – Glycemic Index of 36

Maltitol is very similar to actual sugar in terms of mouth feel, taste, and even cooking performance (except for browning, which it cannot do). It's 90% as sweet with half the calories, so manufacturers love using copious amounts of maltitol in sugar-free desserts and other products.

That's all well and good while you're eating the stuff, but what about half an hour later once all that sugar alcohol has finally reached your colon and the bacteria has started feasting and fermenting?

Bloating, diarrhea, abdominal pain.

It's right there in the name, isn't it? Mal.

There are others, but those are the big ones. Overall, the literature shows that sugar alcohols are fairly neutral as far as blood glucose and insulin effects go. Some people may see spikes, as I've seen reports on blogs and in comment boards to that effect, but most people won't. They can hit your gut pretty hard and cause problems there, especially if you've got a pre-existing condition, but healthy people with healthy digestion (which isn't as widespread as most people think, of course) should be okay with some here and there. Xylitol in particular seems promising, and I'll keep my eye out for more information on that as it emerges.

If you're doing fine without sweeteners (non-caloric, hypo-caloric, artificial, natural, whatever), keep it up.

Don't go looking for an excuse to introduce sugar substitutes.

But if your desire for something, anything sweet is derailing your attempts at a healthy diet, sugar alcohols may be worth experimenting with. Give it a shot if you're gonna and let me know how it goes.

What have your experiences been with sugar alcohols? They get a bad rap from being used in so many processed "low-carb" treats, but have they helped or hindered your path to health?"

Here's a list of some popular sugar alcohols so you can identify them when you look at a nutrition label:
Erythritol
Maltitol
Hydrogenated starch hydrolysates
Isomalt
Lactitol
Mannitol
Sorbitol
Xylitol
Methanol or aspartame

Aspartame/methanol (unknown source maybe from my files)

Aspartame is most often labelled as containing phenylalanine.
Aspartame is made up of aspartic acid and phenylalanine. The latter has been synthetically altered to carry a methyl group, which is responsible for aspartame's sweet taste. The phenylalanine methyl bond, called methyl ester, allows the methyl group on the phenylalanine to easily break off and form methanol.

In fruits and vegetables, methanol is bonded to a fiber called pectin that allows it to be safely passed through your digestive tract. However, in aspartame, methanol is not bonded into anything that can help eliminate it from your body.

Once inside your body, the methanol is converted by alcohol dehydrogenase (ADH) enzyme into formaldehyde, which can wreak havoc on your DNA and sensitive proteins.

All animals, except humans, possess the ability to break down methanol into formic acid.

Methanol, also known as wood alcohol, is found in antifreeze and rocket fuel, among many other applications.

Methanol's effect on the body is similar in some ways to that of ethanol (the alcohol found in wine and beer), but unlike ethanol, the body deals with methanol by transforming it into waste products that include formaldehyde, a carcinogen that morticians use as embalming fluid.

If aspartame delivers methanol to your bloodstream, it would seem like a no-brainer to avoid the sweetener at all costs, but there's a confounding factor: methanol is also found in all sorts of harmless foods, especially fruits and vegetables, in quantities comparable to foods that contain aspartame. In fact, aspartame-flavored soda contains less than half the methanol found in the same volume of many fruit juices.

This is where the dialogue gets contentious. To some researchers, it's clear that methanol is harmless in the small quantities derived from aspartame-containing foods.

However, a study conducted in 2005 by the European Ramazzini Foundation, which tracked the health of aspartame-fed rats for their entire natural lives, linked aspartame consumption with an increased lifetime cancer risk.

Some researchers, as well as the U.S. Food and Drug Administration, found fault with the study's methods, while other scientists rushed to defend it, saying that at the very least, aspartame requires continued examination.

At the heart of the debate is the fact that in rats, as in humans, a large percentage of individuals will succumb to cancer in very old age.

It's difficult for scientists to say whether cancer in a very old rat was caused by lifetime ingestion of a substance such as aspartame, or whether the cancer would have occurred naturally.

As I mentioned in the Introduction, there are other medical conditions that people may also have with their FM issue and some that I was unaware of until I wrote my second cookbook.

Here are just three more little known medical conditions that other people with FM have to deal with;

OXALATES AND SALICYLATES:
http://www.pkdiet.com/pdf/oxalat e%20lists.pdf

"Some folks are particularly bothered by oxalates and salicylates, which are plant chemicals and yet, if they were to ask their physicians about them, would find no answers concerning them.

Oxalates are chemicals in plants (and some animal foods) that bind with minerals in the body, such as magnesium, potassium, calcium, and sodium, creating oxalate salts.

Most of these salts are soluble and pass quickly out of the body. However, oxalates that bind with Calcium are practically insoluble and these crystals solidify in the kidneys (kidney stones) or the urinary tract, causing pain and irritation. Oxalates, as far as I know, are not used in products but as flavourings for recipes. One spice is Cinnamon that is a very high oxalate spice with over 38 mg of oxalate for just one teaspoon. Choose instead cinnamon oil or cinnamon extract.

Cinnamon oil is available from various outlets that sell culinary oils. You can get cinnamon extract in the supplement section of your grocery or health food store – generally, it is sold in capsules. When cooking with it, you simply open the capsules and put the powdered extract into your dish. Substitute about the equivalent amount of dry extract for ground cinnamon. (Not sure about here in Australia).

Salicylates are natural chemicals found in plants that protect the plant from being eaten by insects or attacked by disease. Although poisonous, salicylates are usually tolerated when ingested in small amounts, but when ingested too frequently, they can cause a wide range of symptoms. Salicylates are found to a higher degree in unripe food. This poses problems for Americans, as our food is often picked way too early.

Salicylates are used to make prepared foods, hygiene (toothpaste, lotion, soap, etc.), cosmetic, and drug (Aspirin and others) products, which we are also using more and more of".

For confidentiality reasons, I have edited the next section for this book.

FOOD INTOLERANCE NETWORK FACTSHEET

https://fedup.com.au/factsheets/additive-and-natural-chemical-factsheets/amines

AMINES

Introduction

All foods are made up of hundreds of naturally occurring compounds that can have varying effects on us, depending on how much we eat and how sensitive we are.

Biogenic amines are formed by the breakdown of proteins in foods. They can affect mental functioning, blood pressure, body temperature, and other bodily processes. Some hormones, such as adrenaline (epinephrine) are compounds containing an amine. There are many different amines, including:
☐tyramine (e.g. in cheese)
☐histamine (e.g. in wine)

☐phenylethylamine (e.g. in chocolate)
☐agmatine, putrescine, cadaverine, spermidine (e.g. in decomposing fish)
☐tryptamine
☐adrenaline (ephinephrine)
☐serotonin
☐dopamine

Biogenic amines are normally quickly broken down in the body with the help of enzymes such as MAO (monoamine oxidase-A) which render them harmless. Missing, sluggish or blocked enzymes can lead to a build up of amines in the body.

The 'cheese effect'. In people who are taking certain drugs known as MAOIs (monoamine oxidase inhibitors), the enzyme is inhibited and a build up of tyramine can occur, leading to life-threatening high blood pressure as well as a range of symptoms including headaches, itchy skin rashes, heart palpitations and diarrhoea. A number of MAOI patients died from strokes or heart attacks before doctors realised that patients taking MAOIs needed to avoid foods high in tyramine.

This is called the 'cheese effect' because it was recognised in the 1960s by a British pharmacist who noticed that his wife developed a headache every time she ate cheese - high in tyramine - while taking MAOI antidepressants.

Lacking the enzyme. There is a rare condition in which people who are born without the MAOA gene lack the MAO enzyme.

Researchers have long known that this condition is associated with aggression in men.

Low activity enzyme. Much more common is a low activity variant of the gene known as MAOA-L, which seems to occur in about one third of the population. A study with nine uncontrollable children in 1985 found that on average there was five times more para-cresol in their faeces than for a control group.

Para-cresol is a breakdown product of tyramine. Could it be that these children were failing to metabolise dietary tyramine due to a sluggish enzyme? We don't know because the study was never followed up, although the researchers commented that 'the results point to dietary involvement'.

In 2002, a study found that men with MAOA-L who had been badly treated as children were more likely to exhibit antisocial behaviour than those who had been well treated.

Amines and specific symptoms

Behaviour

Behavioural effects fit with what we see in the Food Intolerance Network. Children with oppositional defiance are the ones whose parents are often told 'he just needs a good smack'. But smacking has the opposite effect – if you smack these kids, when they are big enough they will hit you back. Or if they are scared of their parents, they will hit other people, and this is defined as conduct disorder. You have to treat these kids as if they are your friend – a calm approach – and avoid backing them into a corner at all times. It can be difficult to maintain a calm approach with someone who is extremely aggressive, and experts acknowledge that this approach has limited success. Network members find that it is easier to avoid the food chemicals that cause these effects.

Research suggests that about 70 per cent of children with behaviour problems are affected by salicylates, artificial colours and preservatives, compared to only about 40 per cent affected by amines. Many mothers have reported that their child becomes silly and hyperactive on salicylates whereas amines make them aggressive. In our experience, children who are expelled from day care centres due to aggressive behaviour are usually sensitive to amines as well as to other food chemicals.

Migraines, depression and other symptoms

Amines have been associated with migraines and headaches, as well as other symptoms of food intolerance, including irritable bowel symptoms, eczema and depression.

A possible link with schizophrenia

A biogenic amine called dimethyltriptamine (DMT for short) is the only known hallucinogenic compound naturally produced by the body. Normally it is metabolised by the monoamine oxidase enzyme before its effects can be noticed.

It is used in tribal and religious rites in South America by combining a naturally rich source of DMT with a natural MAO inhibitor while avoiding tyramine containing foods, usually through fasting. DMT is present in small amounts in a wide range of animal and plant foods and mushrooms. In the 1950s, researchers suggested that the schizoid symptoms of auditory or visual hallucinations could be due to an inborn deficit in the MAO enzyme, allowing small amounts of DMT from foods to build up in the body. This theory is once again becoming popular. It would account for why some failsafers have reported that schizoid symptoms improve on a low chemical elimination diet.

Amine levels in different foods

Fish, cheese, wine, some meats, some fruit such as bananas and avocados, some vegetables such as mushrooms, and fermented foods such as chocolate, sauerkraut and soy sauce are just some of the foods that have been listed as containing varying levels of amines, but basically any protein food can contain amines depending on the way it is handled.

The amine content of foods varies greatly due to differences in processing, age, ripeness, handling, storage, variety of grapes or other produce, cooking method and many other factors.

An Australian analysis of the amine contents of fish-based oriental sauces found up to 6 times the legal limit of histamines in some of the samples. Freshness is a key factor for avoiding amines. The new method of meat distribution in our supermarkets is a problem for amine responders. All meat is now vacuum packed, repacked and sold as fresh which means it can be up to ten weeks old when you eat it.

Studies show that vacuum packing can inhibit the growth of bacteria but does nothing to retard the development of amines.

Many drugs can contain amines, including over the counter cold tablets, decongestants, nasal drops or sprays, some pain relievers, general and local anaesthetics and some antidepressants.

In 1996, researchers in a medical journal reported a more user-friendly MAOI diet based on laboratory analyses, claiming that many dietary restrictions were not necessary. Doctors on an internet forum were reluctant about advising patients to relax their diets. 'It is easy but is it safe?' asked one.

Another reported a patient whose diet infringement with a now supposedly safe food resulted in headaches, high blood pressure and seizures.

Experience suggests that people who are sensitive to amines need to know a lot of about the history and freshness of their foods and approach all possible amine-containing foods with caution. Lists of amine-containing foods (such as the one on the World Headache Alliance website) are not complete from our point of view. People with migraines who have avoided some amine-rich foods often say 'I tried avoiding foods and it didn't work'. This is because migraines can be provoked by many other amine-containing foods and/or other food chemicals such as additives, salicylates and glutamates.

AMINE INTOLERANCE OR ALLERGY: WHAT ARE THE SYMPTOMS?
http://whatcanieat.com.au/a/amines--salicylates/amine-intolerance-or-allergy-what--are-the-symptoms-

Let`s start by looking at what Amines are

Amines are naturally occurring chemicals found in many foods. They result from the breakdown of proteins or through the fermentation process, and are responsible for giving the food its flavour. The more intense the flavour, the higher the amine content, so the longer, say, a fruit ripens or a meat cures the more amines it will contain. The highest amounts can be found in aged cheeses, chocolate, wine, many alcoholic beverages, aged meats such as sausage or salami, canned or smoked fish, banana, avocado, and tomato. Amine content increases as certain fruits ripen and as meats and fish age, so those sensitive should only consume the freshest produce, meats and fish.

When you eat a food high in amines, the histamine it contains is metabolised by enzymes and bacteria to amines which are quickly absorbed in the gut and, in people who are sensitive, an allergy-type of response occurs.

The end result is widening of blood vessels, tissue inflammation and swelling just as our own natural histamine creates.

Amine Intolerance or Allergy: What are the Symptoms?

Symptoms of an amine allergy or amine intolerance usually depend on the amount of amine you eat you are likely to tolerate smaller amounts than larger amounts and occur when the enzymes responsible for breaking down histamine are saturated, or used up. The most common symptoms experienced by those sensitive to amines are recurrent eczema and hives, headaches or migraines, sinus trouble, mouth ulcers, fatigue (frequently feeling rundown and tired for no apparent reason), nausea, stomach pains, joint pain that is undiagnosed and digestive issues.

Children can become irritable, restless and exhibit symptoms related to ADHD.

Breast fed babies can exhibit colic, diaper rash, loose stools, and eczema through the milk if the mother is taking in excessive amounts of amines.

If you know that you have reactions to wines, aged cheeses or chocolate, there's a good chance you may be reacting to other foods high in amines. Take them out of your diet completely for a few weeks and see how you feel. If you do have sensitivity to amines, you'll want to limit the amount you eat every day, and determine what your own personal tolerance is to these highly reactive chemicals".

I know that there are a multitude of other well-known medical conditions and many more unknown medical conditions that require special diets; however, I am lucky in many ways that I only have FM to deal with along with the Diabetes, Irritable Bowel Syndrome and Depression.

If I keep my Fructose under control; then I can usually keep the other three conditions under control as well.

Again I state and please remember that I am not qualified in any field of medicine or nutrition and can only share my findings with you for many of the foods that I eat and these sites have similar information as other sites have.

Please listen to your own professional advisors and your own body and make sure that you seek the proper advice and not do a self-diagnosis because of the information that I have provided.

GLUTAMATES

Here are a couple of snippets from two good sites that I was able to get a lot of information from and I do suggest that you visit them.

**http://www.everydaynutrition.com.
au/blog/understanding-food-
chemicals-failsafe**

Glutamates are an amino acid and a part
of all proteins. In foods they may be
found attached to a protein or in their
"free" form. When they are found in
their free form they enhance the flavour
in food. Foods rich in natural glutamates
like cheese, tomato, mushrooms and
meat/yeast extracts are often used to
flavour cooking, and MSG (pure
monosodium glutamate) is used as an
additive in savoury snack foods, soups
and Asian cooking.

**https://www.agribusiness.school.nz
/pluginfile.php/1311/mod_resource
/content/0/factsheet_7_amines_in
_foods%5B1%5D.pdf**

Glutamate is found in many foods in a
natural protein-bound form. It is
important in the enjoyable flavour of
tomatoes, aged cheese and mushrooms,
and most notably found in a Japanese

seaweed sauce from which MSG was extracted. Glutamate is the most common neurotransmitter in the brain; that is, it is responsible for transporting chemical signals from neuron to neuron. However, if the level of glutamates is too high, neurons can misfire, causing physical and psychological problems, and in extreme cases, permanent damage.

LACTOSE INTOLERANCE

The following information comes from: https://www.nhs.uk/Conditions/ lactose-intolerance/Pages/ Causes.aspx

CAUSES OF LACTOSE INTOLERANCE

Lactose intolerance is usually the result of your body not producing enough lactase.

Lactase is an enzyme (a protein that causes a chemical reaction to occur) normally produced in your small intestine that's used to digest lactose.

If you have a lactase deficiency, it means your body doesn't produce enough lactase.

Digesting Lactose

After eating or drinking something containing lactose, it passes down your oesophagus (gullet) into your stomach, where it's digested. The digested food then passes into your small intestine.

The lactase in your small intestine should break lactose down into glucose and galactose (other types of sugar), which are then absorbed into your bloodstream. If there isn't enough lactase, the unabsorbed lactose moves through your digestive system to your colon (large intestine).

Bacteria in the colon ferment (break down) the lactose, producing fatty acids and gases such as carbon dioxide, hydrogen and methane. The breakdown of the lactose in the colon, and the resulting acids and gases that are produced, cause the symptoms of lactose intolerance such as flatulence and bloating.

Types of Lactase deficiency

The main types of lactase deficiency are outlined below.

Primary lactase deficiency

Primary lactase deficiency is the most common cause of lactose intolerance worldwide. This type of lactase deficiency is caused by an inherited genetic fault that runs in families.

Primary lactase deficiency develops when your lactase production decreases as your diet becomes less reliant on milk and dairy products.

This is usually after the age of two, when breastfeeding or bottle-feeding has stopped, although the symptoms may not be noticeable until adulthood.

Secondary lactase deficiency

Secondary lactase deficiency is a shortage of lactase caused by a problem in your small intestine.

It can occur at any age, and may be the result of another condition, surgery to your small intestine, or taking certain medication.

Secondary lactase deficiency is the most common cause of lactose intolerance in the UK, particularly in babies and young children.

Possible causes of secondary lactase deficiency include:
Gastroenteritis – an infection of the stomach and intestines

Coeliac disease – a bowel condition caused by an adverse reaction to a protein called gluten.

Crohn's disease – a long-term condition that causes inflammation of the lining of the digestive system

Ulcerative colitis – a long-term condition that affects the large intestine

Chemotherapy – a cancer treatment

Long courses of antibiotics

The decrease in the production of lactase in secondary lactase deficiency is sometimes only temporary, but it may be permanent if it's caused by a long-term condition. It's also possible to develop secondary lactase deficiency later in life, even without another condition to trigger it. This is because your body's production of lactase naturally reduces as you get older.

Congenital lactase deficiency

Congenital lactase deficiency is a rare condition that runs in families and is found in newborn babies. It's caused by an inherited genetic fault that means affected babies produce very little or no lactase.

The genetic mutation responsible for congenital lactase deficiency is passed on in an autosomal recessive inheritance pattern. This means both parents must have a copy of the faulty gene to pass on the condition.

Developmental lactase deficiency
Some babies born prematurely (before the 37th week of pregnancy) have a temporary lactose intolerance because their small intestine wasn't fully developed by the time they were born. This is known as developmental lactase deficiency and it usually improves as affected babies get older.

Although milk and foods made from milk are the only natural sources of lactose, lactose often is "hidden" in prepared foods to which it has been added. People with very low tolerance for lactose should know about the many food products that may contain lactose, even in small amounts.

Food products that may contain lactose include:
Bread, Baked goods, Processed breakfast cereals, Instant potatoes, soups, and breakfast drinks, Margarine, Lunch meats (except those that are kosher), Salad dressings, Candies, Chips and other processed snacks, Mixes for pancakes,

biscuits, and cookies, Soft cheeses, Milk, Non-dairy whipped toppings, Non-dairy liquid and powered coffee creamers.

Smart shoppers learn to read food labels with care, looking not only for milk and lactose in the contents but also for such words as whey, curds, milk by-products, dry milk solids, and nonfat dry milk powder. If any of these are listed on a label, the item contains lactose.

In addition to food sources, lactose can be "hidden" in medicines. Lactose is used as the base for many prescription and over-the-counter medications. Many types of birth control pills, for example, contain lactose, as do some tablets used for stomach acid and gas. However, these products typically affect only people with severe lactose intolerance because they contain such small amounts of lactose.

The hydrogen breath test is the most convenient and reliable test for lactose intolerance. (Read more about it on the web site mentioned)

IN DEPTH INFORMATION ABOUT GLUTEN INTOLERANCE
https://www.foodintol.com/wheat-gluten-sensitivity/gluten-intolerance-symptoms

Why Does Gluten Cause These Symptoms?

These illnesses and medical conditions are caused by a protein in the grass grain - known as gluten - or more precisely - the protein breakdown fragments of gluten.

Gluten is a very big molecule - in fact it is one of the most complex proteins eaten by man. To be digested it needs to break down many times and many of us do not have the right biological equipment to achieve its full digestion. Our bodies were not 'designed' to digest grass grains like wheat.

The animals which have the perfect and ideal digestive systems for grass grains are birds.

Yes, grazing animals like cows eat grass - but they have evolved four stomachs to do the job

Gluten is very difficult to digest

Some digestion begins in the mouth where the wheat product is chewed and munched and mixed with enzymes in the saliva. This physically breaks up the food before it is swallowed and enters the stomach.

The actual protein breakdown begins in the stomach.

In gluten sensitive people (those who are unable to digest gluten) the effects can first be felt in the duodenum - the very first part of the intestine, right after the stomach. You might feel a "bloating" sensation happening right after a meal - located right under the ribs and above your waist.

But - as many people know too well - there are other symptoms still to come.

The first split-up of the huge gluten protein produces two smaller types of protein - known as peptides:
•Gliadins
•Glutenins

Unfortunately - for people who are gluten intolerant - this is where all the problems begin. Gliadins and glutenins behave in quite different ways - but when working together can have devastating effects on the human body.

While the gliadins work to perforate the intestine and create chaos (like inflammation and disrupted processes) - glutenins get a free ride into the bloodstream via the damaged intestine - and initiate other mischief.

How Gluten Damages the Intestine
Two Protein Breakdown Products of Gluten:

1). Gliadins

One breakdown product of gluten - gliadins - can have a very damaging effect on the intestine. In fact, because of this, gluten is regarded by some as "the protein with teeth" - because this gliadin actually tears holes in the intestinal wall tissue.

Now this may not sound too bad. Everything heals pretty quickly, right?

However the small intestine is where two vital functions take place - absorption and filtering.

ABSORPTION of food nutrients takes place in the small intestine. Food is converted into energy so we can live and breathe and work. And we need the right mix of nutrients and water for every organ and system to operate properly. When absorption goes wrong - we miss out on nutrients and develop dehydration, mineral deficiencies or other conditions which can turn into chronic diseases like anaemia, colitis, arthritis or osteoporosis.

FILTERING (SCREENING) The small intestine also acts as a screening mechanism. It prevents unwanted things like bacteria, fungals and foreign proteins from entering our bloodstream. But when this filter gets holes in it - (with gluten damage you can actually see damaged tissue under a microscope) - all kinds of foreign particles escape into the bloodstream and travel anywhere in the body: the joints, organs, skin and brain.

Of course the brilliant human body heals itself fairly quickly after one-off damage events. However - we usually eat grain-based foods several times a day: breakfast cereals, sandwiches, muffins, cookies, bowls of noodles and pasta. Therefore if you are gluten intolerant - your small intestine does not get the chance to heal. And years and years of such damage eventually leads to diagnosis of chronic disease.

2). Glutenins

The other breakdown peptide of gluten is glutenin. This peptide is responsible for strengthening bread dough and allows loaves to remain raised and 'light' for eating. However gliutenins are also associated with addictive symptoms: cravings, binge eating and addictive behaviour.

Can you now see why your small intestine is such a vital part of your body - and why intestinal health is so central to good health?

The Gluten Protein

Gluten is an enormous and complex protein molecule contained in these grains and others: Wheat, rye, barley and oats. Gluten is in all types of Wheat grain like whole grain wheat, wheat bran, spelt, triticale and others.

Therefore Gluten is also available in everything made out of the flour of these grains: baked foods like bread, pies, cake, breakfast cereals, oatmeal (porridge), cookies, pizza and pasta.

Thousands of processed foods have Gluten in them.

I have very little on what food sources have Gluten; however, I do know that here in Australia, you can't get Gluten Free oats because the oats contain avenin.

A snippet from http://kiallafoods.com.au/gluten-free-oats/ explains
"As they explain it, the term 'gluten' is generally used to describe a prolamin protein fraction that is associated with coeliac disease. This prolamin protein occurs in wheat, barley, rye and oats. However in each of the grains the protein goes by different names: gliadin in wheat, hordein in in barley, secalin in rye, and avenin in oats.

So, in fact, all oats naturally contain the prolamin protein, generally known as gluten, albeit in a slightly different form".

Now you know a little bit more about the issues that I am trying explain to you, I am going to let you know that the Breath Test is done for many other medical conditions beside these and one of them is Diabetes.

My knowledge for what's in what food source has grown immensely since I first began to write my Helpful Dietary Recipes For Most Intolerances cookbooks. I am now going to give you my food chart so that you may endeavour to source out the foods that you can eat and maybe shed a light on what you can't tolerate.

If my information is wrong, it will be because the site where I got my information from is wrong. Sites can be conflicting with their information but at least I have tried my best to inform you and me.

I have tried to source out whether the ingredients have Fructose, Fructans, Polyols or Galactans in them and have indicated this beside the ingredient.

Salicylates, Oxalates, Amines and MSG may also be issues for some people so I have added them as well.

I have split the chart up into sections because Dairy and Meat don't have Fructose, Fructans, Polyols or Galactans and will also be in alphabetical order.

I will explain this chart in more detail in the next chapter.

I also have very little for the Lactose Intolerant people; however, I was always told that the lower the sugar content of the cheese means the lower amount of Lactose that is in it and the higher the fat content in cream, the lower the Lactose

THE FOOD CHARTS EXPLANATION PAGE

These food charts are meant for 'most intolerances' and these are just a few that I have found out about and are often associated with some form of Fructose Malabsorption. There will be many more intolerances out there that I don't know of, so you will have to be the judge of what ingredients you eat.

I am going to use the following code system against ingredients as full charts for fruit, vegetables, herbs and spices would be very hard to read as some of them have all the following in them for example:

Mushrooms have VLOX (very low oxalates), MS (medium salicylates), HAM (high amines), VHMSG (very high glutamates), HF (high Fructose), FOS (Fructans), PO (Polyol) (mannitol & xylitol) and GOS (Galactans) (raffinose)

Bananas have MOX (medium oxalates), LS (low salicylates), MAM (medium amines), MSG (glutamates), MF (medium Fructose), FOS (Fructans) (inulin), PO (Polyol) (sorbitol) and GOS (Galactans) (raffinose)

Fructose – F, Fructans – FOS, Polyols – PO, Galactans – GOS

Low – L, Medium – M, High – H, Very High – VH, Salicylates – S, Oxalates – OX, Amines – AM, Glutamates – MSG

Foods with Sulphites, Benzoates and Monosodium glutamate will be noted as MSG

If one of the above is not listed, it will mean that the food item has either not been tested or it doesn't have it in it. There may be "EX" before the food item and that means that it is extremely high. MH means medium – high.

This chart is the best way for me to tell you what's in what without having to make another big book that would be very awkward for you to carry around with you if you wanted to.

I will start with the bigger charts and then to the smaller charts that don't have the Fructose, Fructans, Polyols and Galactans in them, like the dairy, meat and seafood. There is also a "Miscellaneous" list where I have placed a few foods that I either didn't know where to place them, or they had extra intolerances against them for the smaller charts.

VEGETABLES

Acorn Squash	VLOX, S, AM, F, FOS, PO
Alfalfa Sprouts	LOX, S, LAM,HF, FOS
Artichokes	MOX, HS, LAM, HF, HFOS
Avocado	VLOX, HS, HAM, MSG, F, FOS, PO (sorbitol)
Asparagus	LOX, MS, LAM, HF, FOS, PO (mannitol), GOS (raffinose)
Bamboo Shoots	LOX, LS, LAM, FOS
Bean Sprouts	LOX, LS, F, FOS
Beets (beetroot)	VHOX, MS, LAM, MSG, HF, FOS, PO (mannitol), GOS (raffinose)
Bok Choy	VLOX, MS, LAM, FOS, PO (sorbitol), GOS (raffinose)
Broad Beans	HOX, S, HAM, F, FOS, PO (sorbitol), GOS (raffinose)

Broccoli Tips-Boiled	LOX, HS, HAM, VHMSG, HF, FOS, PO (mannitol / sorbitol), GOS (raffinose)
Broccoli-Boiled	LOX, HS, HAM, VHMSG, HF, FOS, PO (mannitol / sorbitol), GOS (raffinose)
Broccoli-Raw	MOX, HS, HAM, VHMSG, HF, FOS, PO (mannitol / sorbitol), GOS (raffinose)
Broccoli-Steamed	HOX, HS, HAM, VHMSG, HF, FOS, PO (mannitol / sorbitol), GOS (raffinose)
Brussel Sprouts-Boiled	LOX, LS, LAM, HF, HFOS, PO (sorbitol), HGOS (raffinose)

Brussel Sprouts-Raw	MOX, LS, LAM, HF, HFOS, PO (sorbitol), HGOS (raffinose)
Brussel Sprouts-Steamed	HOX, LS, LAM, HF, HFOS, PO (sorbitol), HGOS (raffinose)
Butternut Squash / pumpkin	VLOX, S, AM, HF, FOS, PO (mannitol), GOS
Cabbage, Green-Boiled	LOX,.LS, LAM, HF, FOS, PO (sorbitol), HGOS (raffinose)
Cabbage, Green-Raw	LOX, LS, LAM, HF, FOS, PO (sorbitol), HGOS (raffinose)
Cabbage, Green-Steamed	MOX, LS, LAM, HF, FOS, PO (sorbitol), HGOS (raffinose)
Cabbage, Red	LOX, LS, LAM, HF, FOS, PO (sorbitol), HGOS (raffinose)
Cabbage - savoy	LOX, LS, LAM, HF, FOS, PO (sorbitol), HGOS (raffinose)

Canned Vegetables	Varies OX, Varies S, LAM, LMSG, PO (aspartame)
Capsicum red	LOX, VHS, LAM, HF, FOS, PO (sorbitol), GOS
Capsicum green	MOX, VHS, LAM, HF, FOS, PO (sorbitol), GOS
Capsicum yellow	MOX, VHS, LAM, HF, FOS, PO (sorbitol), GOS
Carrots-Boiled	MOX, HS, LAM, MSG, HF, FOS, PO (sorbitol), GOS (raffinose)
Carrots-Raw	VHOX, HS, LAM, MSG, HF, FOS, PO (sorbitol), GOS (raffinose)
Carrots-Steamed	VHOX, HS, LAM, MSG, HF, FOS, PO (sorbitol), GOS (raffinose)

Cauliflower-Boiled	VLOX, MS, VHAM, MSG, F, FOS, PO (sorbitol/ mannitol), GOS (raffinose)
Cauliflower-Raw	LOX, MS, VHAM, MSG, F, FOS, PO (sorbitol/ mannitol), GOS (raffinose)
Cauliflower-Steamed	LOX, MS, VHAM, MSG, F, FOS, PO (sorbitol/ mannitol), GOS (raffinose)
Celeriac	HOX, VLAM, F, FOS, PO (mannitol)
Celery-Raw	VHOX, LS, LAM, MSG, HF, FOS, PO (mannitol), GOS
Chard	VHOX, VHAM, F, FOS, PO (sorbitol)
Chili Peppers	HOX, HS, LAM, F, PO (mannitol)
Chili powder/ flakes/sauce	LOX, VHS, F, PO (mannitol)
Chinese Broccoli/ gai lan	HS, VHAM, VHMSG, FOS GOS (raffinose)

Chinese Spinach/ kang kong	VHS, HAM, HMSG, FOS GOS (raffinose)
Chinese pak choy	HS, HAM, HMSG, FOS GOS (raffinose)
Chinese gai choy must green	VHS, HAM, FOS, GOS (raffinose)
Chinese wombok	HS, HAM, MSG, FOS GOS (raffinose)
Chinese Choy sum	VHS, HAM, MSG, FOS, PO, GOS
Choko	LOX, LS, LAM, LMSG, HF, FOS, PO (mannitol)
Collard Greens boiled	MOX, LAM, HF, PO (sorbitol)
Collard Greens- Raw	LOX, LAM, HF, PO (sorbitol)
Collard Greens- Steamed	HOX, LAM, HF, PO (sorbitol)
Corn	LOX, MS, MAM, VHMSG, HF, FOS, PO (xylitol), GOS
Cucumbers/peeled	VLOX, HS, LAM, HF, FOS, PO (sorbitol), GOS

Eggplant	MOX, HS, HAM, F, FOS, PO (xylitol)
Garlic	LOX, LS, VHMSG, F, FOS GOS (raffinose)
Gherkin pickled	VHS, HAM, HF, FOS, PO (sorbitol), GOS
Green Beans	VLOX, MS, VLAM, HF, FOS, PO (sorbitol), GOS
Kale	MOX, LS, LAM, F, FOS, PO (sorbitol), GOS (raffinose)
Karela/bitter gourd	AM, MSG, HFOS, MGOS
Kohlrabi	VLOX, LS, LAM, PO
Leek	MOX, LS, LAM, F, HFOS, HPO (mannitol), GOS
Lettuce any other (1/2 cup)	MOX, MS, LAM, HF, FOS, PO (sorbitol), GOS
Lettuce, Iceberg (1/2 cup)	LOX, LS, LAM, MF, FOS, PO, GOS
Lettuce, Iceberg, (1 cup)	LOX, MS, LAM, MF, FOS, PO, GOS

Lettuce Romaine (1/2 cup)	MOX, MS, LAM, MF, FOS, PO, GOS
Lettuce, Romaine (1 cup)	MOX, MS, LAM, F, FOS, PO, GOS
Marrow	MS, LAM, FOS, PO
Mung Bean Sprouts	LOX, LS, LAM, FOS
Mushrooms (normal)	VLOX, MS, HAM, VHMSG, HF, FOS, PO (mannitol & xylitol), GOS (raffinose)
Mushrooms shiitake	VHS, HAM, MSG, F, PO (mannose)
Mushrooms enoki	VHS, HAM, MSG, VLPO (mannose)
Mushrooms oyster	VHS, VHAM, VHMSG, VLPO (mannose)
Mushrooms king oyster	VHS, VHAM, VHMSG, VLPO (mannose)
Mushrooms reishi	VHS, VHAM, VHMSG, VLPO (mannose)

Mushrooms maitake	VHS, VHAM, VHMSG, VLPO (mannose)
Okra	VHOX, HS, LAM, HF, HFOS, PO (xylitol), GOS
Onions white & yellow	LOX, LS, LAM, MSG, HF, HFOS (inulin), PO (mannitol), GOS
Onions red	MOX, MS, HAM, HF, HFOS, PO (mannitol), GOS
Parsnips	HS, LAM, F, LFOS, PO
Peas-Boiled	VLOX, LS, LAM, MSG, HF, HFOS, PO, GOS (raffinose)
Peas, green, fresh or frozen	LOX, LS, LAM, MSG, F, FOS, PO, GOS (raffinose)
Peppers, Green	MOX, VHS, HAM, VHMSG, HF, FOS, PO (sorbitol), GOS

Peppers, Red	VLOX, VHS, HAM, VHMSG, HF, FOS, PO (sorbitol), GOS
Peppers yellow	MOX, VHS, HAM, VHMSG, HF, FOS, PO (sorbitol), GOS
Pepper Aleppo pul biber	VLOX, LS, HAM, MSG, HF, FOS, PO (sorbitol), GOS
Pepper Jalapenos	VHS, HAM, HMSG, HF, FOS, PO (sorbitol), GOS
Pickles (Dill)	VLOX, VHS, MAM, F, PO, GOS
Potatoes, Red-Peeled	MOX, MSG, HF, FOS, PO, GOS
Potatoes-Peeled	VHOX, LS, LAM, MSG, HF, FOS, PO, GOS
Potatoes-Unpeeled	VHOX, MS, LAM, MSG, HF, FOS, PO, GOS
Pumpkin-Canned	VLOX, MS, FOS, PO (aspartame), GOS

Pumpkin-Raw	VLOX, MS, HAM, HMSG, MHF, FOS, PO (mannitol)
Radicchio	HS, HAM, HMSG, F, HFOS
Radishes-Red	VLOX, VHS, LAM, HF, FOS, PO
Radishes-White daikon	VLOX, VHS, LAM, HF, PO
Sauerkraut	MOX, MSG, F, FOS, PO
Shallots (white part)	MOX, LS, LAM, MSG, MHF, HFOS, PO (mannitol), GOS
Shallots/spring onion/scallions	MOX, LS, LAM, MSG, MHF, HFOS, PO (mannitol), GOS
Silverbeet	HOX, HS, VHAM, VHMSG, HF, FOS, PO (sorbitol), GOS
Snow peas	MOX, MS, LAM, MSG, HF, HFOS, PO (sorbitol), GOS
Sorrel	HOX, F, FOS, PO

Spaghetti Squash	LS, MAM, HF, HFOS, PO (sorbitol), GOS
Spinach -Fresh	VHOX, HS, HAM, VHMSG, HF, FOS, PO (sorbitol), GOS
Spinach-Frozen	VHOX, MS, VHAM, VHMSG, HF, FOS, PO (sorbitol), GOS
Squash (yellow summer)	HOX, VLAM, HF, FOS, PO (sorbitol)
String Beans	MOX, LS, VLAM, HF, FOS, PO (sorbitol), GOS
Sugar snap peas	HOX, MS, HF, HFOS, PO (mannitol), GOS
Sweet Potatoes	VHOX, HS, LAM, MSG, HF, FOS, PO (mannitol), GOS (raffinose)
Swede	VLOX, LS, LAM, FOS, PO (sorbitol)
Taro	LAM, F, FOS, PO (mannitol), GOS

Tomato juice (canned)	MOX, MS, HAM, MSG, HF, PO (mannitol & aspartame)
Tomato Paste-Canned	HOX, VHS, HAM, MSG, HF, FOS, PO (mannitol & aspartame)
Tomato Purée-Canned	HOX, VHSS, HAM, MSG, HF, FOS, PO (mannitol & aspartame)
Tomato Sauce-Canned	HOX, VHS, HAM, MSG, HF, FOS, PO (mannitol & aspartame)
Tomatoes Sun Dried	HOX, HS, HAM, EXHMSG, HF, FOS, PO (mannitol & aspartame), GOS
Tomatoes canned/tin	H-VHOX, LS, HAM, MSG, HF, FOS, PO (mannitol & aspartame)

Tomato soup	M-HOX, MS, HAM, MSG, HF, FOS, PO (mannitol & aspartame)
Tomatoes-Fresh	MOX, MS, HAM, VHMSG, HF, FOS, PO (mannitol & aspartame)
Turnip	MOX, LS, LAM, MF, LFOS, PO (sorbitol)
Turnip greens	MOX, LS, LAM, HF, PO (sorbitol)
Yams	HOX, HS, LAM, MSG, HF, FOS, PO (mannitol), GOS
Yucca Root/ cassava	HOX, S, F, FOS, GOS
Zucchini	VLOX, VHS, LAM, HF, HFOS, PO (sorbitol), GOS

FRUIT

Apple Juice	VLOX, MS, LAM, F, PO (sorbitol)
Apples-Golden Delicious	LOX, LS, LAM, F, FOS, PO (sorbitol), GOS (raffinose)
Apples-Granny Smith	LOX, HS, LAM, F, FOS, PO (sorbitol), GOS (raffinose)
Apples-Jonathan	LOX, HS, LAM, F, FOS, PO (sorbitol), GOS (raffinose)
Apples-Red Delicious	LOX, MS, LAM, F, FOS, PO (sorbitol), GOS (raffinose)
Apricots-Fresh	VLOX, VHS, LAM, F, FOS, PO (sorbitol), GOS
Bananas	MOX, LS, MAM, MSG, F, FOS (inulin) PO (sorbitol), GOS (raffinose)
Blackberries	VHOX, VHS, VHAM, F, FOS, HPO (sorbitol), GOS

Blueberries	LOX, VHS, LAM, F, HFOS, PO (xylitol)
Boysenberries	VHS, VHAM, HF, PO (mannitol)
Canned Fruits	Varies OX, Varies S, HAM, VHMSG, F, PO (aspartame)
Cantaloupe	VHS, LAM, F, FOS, PO (mannitol), GOS (raffinose)
Casaba (Melon)	LOX, HS, F, FOS, PO (mannitol), GOS (raffinose)
Cherimoya	OX, MS, HAM, F, HFOS, PO, GOS
Cherries-Fresh	VLOX, HS, HAM, HF, PO (sorbitol), GOS
Cherries glazed	HS, HAM, HF, PO (sorbitol)
Coconut	VLOX, HS, HAM, MSG, F, FOS (inulin), PO (sorbitol)
Coconut Flour	LOX, HS, HAM, FOS, PO (sorbitol)

Coconut cream	HS, HAM, HF, FOS, PO (sorbitol)
Coconut Milk	HS, HAM, HF, FOS, PO (sorbitol), GOS
Coconut Oil	LOX, VHS, HAM
Coconut butter	HS, F, FOS
Coconut water	HS, HAM, FOS, PO (sorbitol)
Cranberries dried	MOX, VHS, VHAM, F, PO (mannitol)
Cranberries can (O Spray)	LOX, VHS, VHAM, F, PO
Currants-Black	HOX, VHS, HAM, MHF, PO (mannitol)
Currants-Red	HOX, VHS, HAM, MHF, PO (mannitol)
Custard Apple	OX, MS, LAM, F, HFOS, PO, HGOS
Dates 1 Deglet Noor dried	HOX, VHS, HAM, LF, FOS (maltose), PO
Dates, 1 medjool	HOX, VHS, HAM, HF, FOS (maltose), PO (dried)
Figs-Dried	VHOX, HS, HAM, F, FOS, PO

Figs-Fresh	VHOX, MS, HAM, F, PO
Gooseberries	HOX, VHS, LAM, MSG, F, PO (sorbitol)
Grape Juice-Purple	HS, HAM, MSG, F, PO (sorbitol)
Grape Juice-Red	MOX, HS, HAM, MSG, F, PO (sorbitol)
Grape Juice-White	LOX, MS, HAM, MSG, F, PO (sorbitol)
Grapefruit	HS, HAM, F, HFOS, PO (sorbitol)
Grapefruit Juice	VLOX, HS, HAM, F, PO (sorbitol)
Grapes-Green	VLOX, VHS, HAM, VHMSG, F, PO (sorbitol), GOS
Grapes-Red	LOX, HS, HAM, VHMSG, F, PO (sorbitol), GOS
Guava	VHS, LAM, F, PO (xylitol & sorbitol)

Honeydew	VLOX, HAM, F, FOS, PO
Huckleberries	LOX, VHS, LAM, F, HFOS, PO (xylitol)
Jack Fruit	HS,HAM, HMSG, HF, FOS
Kiwi fruit	VHOX, HS, LAM, MSG, F, PO (sorbitol)
Kumquats	VLOX, HAM, F, PO (sorbitol)
Lemon Juice	LOX, L-HS, HAM, F, PO (sorbitol)
Lemon Peel	HOX, VHAM, MSG, F, PO (sorbitol)
Lemons and lemongrass	VLOX, MS, VHAM, MSG, F, PO (sorbitol)
Lime Juice	LOX, HAM, F, PO (sorbitol)
Lime Peel	HOX,F, PO (sorbitol)
Limes	MOX, LS, MSG, F, PO (sorbitol)
Longons	OX, S, VLAM, HFOS, PO (sorbitol)

Loquats	MS, LAM, F, PO (sorbitol)
Mandarin Oranges	MOX, VHS, VHAM, MSG, F, PO (sorbitol)
Mangos	LOX, MS, MAM, HF, PO (sorbitol), GOS
Mulberry	HS, LAM, F, FOS, PO (mannitol)
Nectarines	HS, LAM, F, FOS, PO (sorbitol)
Olives, Black	VHOX, MS, VHAM, MSG, FOS, PO
Olives, Green	VHOX, HS, VHAM, MSG, F, FOS, PO
Orange Juice-Fresh	VLOX, MS, VHAM, HF, PO (sorbitol)
Orange Juice-Frozen	VLOX, MS, VHAM, HF, PO (sorbitol)
Orange Peel	HOX, VHAM, HF, PO (sorbitol)
Oranges	HOX, VHS, HAM, MSG, HF, PO (sorbitol)

Papayas/pawpaw	MOX, LS, LAM, MSG, F, FOS (dried), PO (xylitol)
Passion Fruit	VLOX, MS, HAM, F, FOS, PO
Peaches	VLOX, HS, LAM, HF, HFOS, HPO (sorbitol/mannitol), GOS
Pears-Peeled	LOX, LS, LAM, VHF, PO (sorbitol), GOS
Pears-Unpeeled	MOX, HS, MAM, VHF, PO (sorbitol), GOS
Persimmons	HOX, MS, LAM, F, HFOS
Pineapple	LOX, VHS, HAM, MSG, F, FOS, PO (sorbitol/mannitol), GOS
Plantains (banana)	HOX, MAM, MMSG, F, FOS (inulin), PO, GOS

Plums	LOX, MS, HAM, VHMSG, F, HPO (sorbitol)
Pomegranate	MOX, HS, VLAM, HF, HFOS, PO (sorbitol), GOS
Prunes	VHS, VHMSG, HF, HPO (sorbitol)
Quinces & paste	MSG, VHF, MFOS
Raisins/sultanas	LOX, VHS, AM, VHMSG, VHF, FOS, PO (sorbitol)
Rambutan	LS, LAM, HF, HFOS, PO
Raspberries-Black	VHOX, VHS, HAM, MSG, F, HFOS, PO (xylitol)
Raspberries-Red	HOX, VHS, VHAM, MSG, F, HFOS, PO (xylitol)
Rhubarb	VHOX, LAM, F, FOS, PO
Rock melon	VHOX, LAM, F, FOS, PO (mannitol), GOS (raffinose)

Strawberries	M-HOX, VHS, HAM, F, PO (xylitol)
Star Fruit	VHOX, S, HF, PO
Sultanas	LOX, VHS, VHAM, VHMSG, F, FOS, PO (sorbitol)
Tamarillo	LS, LAM, F, FOS
Tangelos	VHS, VHAM, F, PO (sorbitol)
Tangerines	VHS, AM, F, PO (sorbitol)
Watermelon	VLOX, HS, LAM, HF, HFOS, PO (mannitol)

HERBS

Basil	MOX, VHS, LAM, F, LFOS, LGOS
Bay Leaf	VHS, FOS
Caraway	HS, MSG
Chives	VLOX, LS, LAM, F, FOS, PO (mannitol), GOS (raffinose)
Coriander/Cilantro	MOX, LS, L-HAM, FOS

Coriander seeds	HOX, L-HAM
Cumin	MOX, VHS, MSG
Cumin seed	HOX, VHS, MSG
Dill	L-MOX, VHS, MSG, F, FOS
Endive	OX, VHS, VLAM, LF, FOS, PO (xylitol)
Fenugreek	MOX, VHS, AM, FOS, PO
Fennel	MOX, LS, VLAM, LF, HFOS, PO (mannitol)
Fennel leaves	OX, S, FOS, PO (mannitol)
Fennel seeds/tea	LOX, M-HS, FOS, PO (mannitol)
Marjoram	LOX, EXHS, MSG, F, FOS
Oregano	HOX, VHS, MSG, F, FOS, PO (mannose), GOS (raffinose)
Parsley	LOX, LS, VLAM, F, FOS, PO (mannitol), GOS (raffinose)

Peppermint	VHS, LAM, PO (xylitol & menthol)
Rosemary	LOX, VHS, LAM, FOS, PO
Sage	LOX, VHS, F, FOS, PO (mannose), GOS (raffinose)
Tarragon	VLOX, VHS, LAM, FOS
Thyme	LOX, VHS, LAM, FOS

SPICES

Allspice	VHS, LAM, MSG
Anise	VHS, HAM, MSG
Asafoetida powder	LAM, VLF
Cardamon	LOX, HS, MSG
Cinnamon	HOX, VHS, MSG, F
Cloves	VHOX, HS, MSG, F
Curry powder	VHS, MSG, F
Ginger	LOX, MS, MSG, F, FOS
Mustard seed (Spice)	VLOX, VHS, VHAM, MSG,F, FOS, GOS

Mustard prepared yellow 1tb	LOX, HS, VHAM, MSG, F
Mustard powder	VLOX, VHS, VHAM, MSG, F, FOS, GOS
Nutmeg	VLOX, VHS, MSG, F, PO (methanol)
Paprika	VHS, VHAM, HF
Pepper, Black (spice)	HOX, VHS, LAM, F
Pepper, White (spice)	VLOX, VHS, HAM, F
Pepper, cayenne	LOX, VHS, HAM, HF
Peppercorn	HOX, VHS, LAM, F
Turmeric	VHOX, VHS, LAM, F, FOS

NUTS AND SEEDS

Almonds	VHOX, VHS, LAM, MSG, F, FOS, PO (xylitol), GOS
Brazil Nuts	HS, F, FOS, GOS
Cashews	VHOX, LS, LAM, LMSG, F, FOS, GOS
Chestnuts	VLOX, HS, HAM, F, FOS, GOS (raffinose)

Hazelnuts (Filberts)	VHOX, MS, MAM, MSG, FOS, GOS
Lychees	LOX, LAM, F, HPO (sorbitol)
Macadamia	VHOX, HS, MSG, FOS
Peanuts	VHOX, VHS, MSG, FOS, GOS (raffinose)
Pecans	VHOX, MS, MAM, MSG, FOS
Pine Nuts	VHOX, HS, HAM, MSG, FOS, GOS
Pistachio Nuts	HOX, HS, HAM,HFOS, GOS
Walnuts	VHOX, HS, VHAM, MSG, GOS
Water Chestnuts	VLOX, VHS, LAM, PO
	SEEDS
Chai seeds	OX, HS, LAM, FOS
Flax Seed	LOX, S, AM, FOS
Poppy seeds	LS, LAM LMSG, F
Pumpkin Seeds	MOX, MS, MAM, MMSG, FOS
Sesame Seeds	VHOX, HS, MAM, MMSG, FOS, GOS

Sunflower seeds	HOX, LS, AM, FOS

BEANS, PEAS, LENTILS AND RICE

Black Beans	VHOX, LS,MSG,F, FOS, PO (sorbitol), GOS (raffinose)
Borlotti beans	LS, HAM, FOS, PO (sorbitol), GOS (raffinose)
Butter Beans	MSG, FOS, PO (sorbitol), GOS (raffinose)
Cannellini Beans	MOX, LS, LAM, LMSG, FOS, PO (sorbitol), GOS (raffinose)
Fava Beans	LS, VHAM, MSG, FOS,GOS
Garbanzo Beans	MOX, LS, MSG, FOS, GOS
Haricot Beans	MS, LAM, MSG, FOS, PO, GOS
Kidney Beans	HOX, LS, LAM, FOS, GOS
Lima Beans	MOX, LS, MSG, F, FOS, GOS (raffinose)
Mung Beans	MOX, LS, FOS, GOS
Navy Beans	VHOX, LS, MSG, HFOS, GOS

Pinto Beans	VHOX, LS, FOS, GOS
PEAS	
Black-Eyed Peas	LOX, LS, LAM, MSG, FOS, PO (sorbitol), GOS (raffinose)
Chick Peas	MOX, LS, LAM, FOS, GOS
LENTILS	
Lentils - Boiled	MOX, LS, LAM, MSG, FOS, GOS
Split Peas-Green	MOX, LS, LAM, MSG, FOS, GOS
Split Peas-Yellow	LOX, LS, LAM, MSG, FOS, GOS
RICE	
Rice-Brown	MOX, LS, LAM, LMSG, FOS
Rice-White	VLOX, LS, LAM, LMSG, F, FOS
Rice - wild	VLOX, LS, LAM, LMSG, F, FOS
Rice Basmati	LOX, MS, LAM, LMSG, FOS
Rice Doongara	LOX, LAM, LMSG, FOS
OTHER	
Couscous	HOX, LAM, LMSG, FOS

Pearl Barley	LOX, LS, LAM, LMSG, HFOS, GOS
Tapioca	LAM, LMSG, FOS

GRAINS, FLOUR AND BAKING

Amaranth (GF)	HOX, LS, LAM, LMSG, FOS, PO (mannose) GOS
Arrowroot	LOX, LS, LAM, LMSG, FOS, GOS
Barley	LOX, LS, LAM, LMSG, F, FOS (maltose), GOS
Bean Flour	Varies OX, VLS, FOS
Buckwheat	VHOX, LS, LAM, LMSG, FOS
Durum	VHOX, LS, LAM, FOS
Kamut	HOX, AM, MSG, LFOS
Millet	VHOX, LS, LAM, LMSG, FOS
Quinoa	HOX, LAM, LMSG, FOS
Rice Flour	LOX, LS, LAM, LMSG, FOS
Rice bran	LS, LAM
Rye	VHOX, LS, LAM, LMSG, HFOS, GOS

Seed Flour	VARIES OX, VARIES S
Sorghum Flour	VHOX, LAM, LMSG, FOS
Soy	VHOX, LS, MSG, FOS, GOS (raffinose)
Soy Lecithin	VLOX, LS, MSG
Spelt	HOX, FOS
Wheat (Gluten)	VHOX, LS, LAM, LMSG, HFOS
Wheat Germ (Gluten)	HOX, LS
Cornmeal/flour	MOX, HS, AM
Cornstarch	MOX, MSG
	BAKING
Baker's Yeast	MOX, LS, MSG
Bare Yeast non- bakers	MOX, VHS, MSG
Baking Powder	VLOX, MSG
Baking Soda	LOX, MSG
Cream of Tartar	VLOX, S, AM
Gelatin (Unflavored)	VLOX, MSG
Guar gum	MSG, PO (mannose), GOS

Vanilla	VLOX, VHS, LAM, F
Vanillin true	VLOX, LAM, F
Xantham Gum	AM, MSG, PO (mannose), GOS

SWEETENERS

Barley malt syrup	MOX, LS, LAM, MSG, F, FOS (maltose)
Corn Syrup	VLOX, HS, MSG, F, FOS (maltose), GOS
Date Sugar	HOX, VHS, AM, MSG, F, FOS (maltose)
Golden Syrup	LS, AM, MSG, F
Honey	VLOX, VHS, AM, HF, FOS (may have Tutin toxin)
Maple Syrup	VLOX, LS, AM, F, PO
Molasses	MS, F
Rice malt syrup	LS, LAM, VLFOS (maltose)

COFFEE, TEA, COCOA

Coffee beans	VLOX, Varies S, AM, F, FOS, PO (mannitol), GOS

Coffee (Instant)	VLOX, Varies S, AM, F, FOS, PO (mannitol), GOS
	TEA
Chamomile tea	LOX, S, FOS, PO (sorbitol), GOS
Dandelion tea	HOX, S, HFOS, PO
Green Tea	M-HOX, VHS, LAM, FOS, PO, GOS
Herbal teas	Varies OX, Varies S, HAM, M-HFOS
Spearmint Tea	VLOX, VHS, AM, F, PO (xylitol)
Tea (normal)	Varies OX, Varies S, FOS, PO (sorbitol)
	COCOA
Chocolate / cacao	VHOX, LS, MSG, HF, FOS, GOS (raffinose)
Cocoa Powder	VHOX, MS, FOS, PO (mannose), GOS (raffinose)
Chickory root/ stems/leaves	VHS, LAM, F, FOS (inulin), M-HPO (mannitol)

Carob	VHOX, LS, MSG, HFOS, GOS

MISCELLANEOUS AND JUICES

Eggs	LOX, LS, LAM, F
Horseradish Sauce	MS, AM, MSG, FOS
Juniper berries	L-MOX, VHS
Kefir	LAM, HMSG, High Lactose
Ketchup	VLOX, VHS, AM, MSG, HF, FOS, PO (mannitol & aspartame)
Miso	HOX, MAM, VHMSG, FOS, GOS
Oats/milk	MOX, LS, LAM, LMSG, FOS, GOS
Poppadum	Varies OX, Varies S
Pasta	Varies OX, Varies S, FOS
Peanut Butter	VHOX, MS, MSG, FOS, GOS (raffinose)
Soy Sauce	LS, AM, MSG, FOS
Tahini	VHOX, HS, AM, FOS, GOS

Tamarind	LS, AM, MSG, HFOS, GOS
Tobacco	OX, S, AM, MSG,F, FOS, PO (methanol)
Watercress	LOX, HS, LAM, F, PO
Rice protein isolate	LS, LAM, Gluten Free
Whey Protein Concentrate	AM, MSG, has Lactose
Whey Protein Isolate	AM, MSG, has Lactose
Worcestershire sauce	HS, MSG, FOS
Yeast extract / vegemite	VHS, MSG
	JUICES
Aloe Vera Juice	VLOX, S, AM, PO
Cherry Juice	LOX, HS, HAM, F, PO
Cranberry Juice	VLOX, VHS, VHAM, F, PO
Evaporated Cane Juice	VLOX, LS, F, PO
Pineapple Juice	VLOX, MS, HAM,F, PO (sorbitol/mannitol)

THE FOOD CHARTS EXPLANATION PAGE FOR DAIRY, MEAT, SEAFOOD AND DAIRY ALTERNATIVES

These food charts are meant for 'most intolerances' and these are just a few that I have found out about and are often associated with some form of Fructose Malabsorption. There will be many more intolerances out there that I don't know of, so you will have to be the judge of what ingredients you eat.

Remember that I am only giving you this reference to try and help you with your food groups and they may not be completely correct because the web sites that I got them from may be different from other sites. I know that there are many more foods that I have not included but I couldn't find any information on them because they may not have been tested yet.

Dairy, meat and seafood don't have Fructose, Fructans, Polyols and Galactans in them; however, some of the dairy alternatives may have so I am leaving the chart in. If the dairy has Lactose in it, then I will state this where possible.

I am going to use the same following code system against ingredients and will add extras at the end of each food if needed.

Low – L, Medium – M, High – H, Very High – VH, Salicylates – S, Oxalates – OX, Amines – AM, Glutamates – MSG

Foods with Sulphites, Benzoates and Monosodium glutamate will be noted as MSG

Fructose – F, Fructans – FOS, Polyols – PO, Galactans – GOS

If one of the above is not listed, it will mean that the food item has either not been tested or it doesn't have it in it.

Here's something to know about cream: the higher the fat content, the lower the lactose content. Half-and-half has just over 4.0% of lactose. Light or table cream runs just under 4.0% of lactose.

Whipping cream (also called light whipping cream) has somewhere between 3.0% and 3.5% of lactose. Heavy cream has about 3.0% of lactose.

With cheese the lower the sugar content, the lower the lactose content.

DAIRY

	CHEESE
Brie	MSG, Low Lactose
Camembert cheese	LS, MSG, Low Lactose
Cheddar cheese	LOX, MAM, Low Lactose
Cheese Fresh, unfermented	LAM, Lactose
Cheese Mild	LAM, Lactose
Colby style cheese	AM, Low Lactose
Cottage, creamed cheese	AM, Low Lactose
Cottage Cheese Fresh	LAM, Lactose
Cream cheese	LAM, Medium Lactose
Danish Blue vein	L-MS, MAM, Low Lactose
Edam	MAM, Low Lactose
Emmental	LAM, Low Lactose
Feta cheese	MAM, Low Lactose
Goat cheese	MAM, Low Lactose
Gouda	LAM, MSG Low Lactose

Gruyere	LAM, MSG, Low Lactose
Haloumi cheese	AM, Medium Lactose
Havarti cheese	AM, Low Lactose
Jarlsberg	LAM, Low Lactose
Leicester	MAM, Lactose
Limberger	MAM, Low Lactose
Mascarpone	LAM, Lactose
Mozzarella cheese	LS, MAM, Low Lactose
Parmesan	LOX, MAM, MSG, Low Lactose
Provolone	MAM, Low Lactose
Pecorino cheese	AM, MSG, Low Lactose
Quark	LAM, Medium Lactose
Ricotta Fresh	LAM, Medium Lactose
Roquefort	MAM, MSG, Lactose
Swiss cheese	MAM, Low Lactose

MILK, CREAM, YOGURT AND MAYONAISE

Milk, cow (any type that is not lactose free)	LAM, High Lactose

Milk, lactose free	LAM, Low Lactose
Milk, Lactose Hydrolyzed	LOX, LAM, Lactose
Milk, a2	Not tested but has High Lactose
Milk, Lactaid	LOX, LAM, Lactose
Milk, goat	LAM, High Lactose
Buttermilk	VLOX, VHS, VHAM, MSG, High Lactose
Cream, pure, regular fat	Medium Lactose
Thickened regular cream	Medium Lactose
Sour cream	HAM, Medium Lactose
Yoghurt (any type that is not lactose free)	VLOX, MAM, Lactose
Yoghurt lactose free	LOX, AM, Low Lactose
Mayonnaise, low or regular fat	L-MOX, MAM, MSG, Low Lactose
Mayonnaise salad dressing	LOX, MAM, MSG

	DAIRY ALTERNATIVES
Milk, Almond	VHS, VHAM, (stated as Low Lactose)
Milk, hemp	VLS, LAM (stated as Low Lactose)
Milk, rice	VLAM
Soy cheese, hard	HAM
Soy cream cheese	MAM
Soy custard	MAM
Soy yogurt	MAM
Milk, soya beans	VHOX, LS, LAM, MSG, FOS, GOS
Tempeh, plain	OX, S, VHAM, VHMSG, HFOS, GOS
Tofu	MOX, LS, LAM, HFOS, GOS

BUTTERS, OILS AND VINEGARS

Butter	VLOX, LAM, LMSG
Nuttelex non-dairy	LS, LAM, LMSG
Ghee	LOX, LAM

Dairy Blend (70% butter, 30% oil)	LOX, Low Lactose but High Fat
Margarine, poly- or monosaturated 70% fat	LOX, LS, AM, MSG, Low Lactose but High Fat
Copha	HS, HAM, High Fat
Seed butters	Varies OX, Varies AM, MSG
OILS	
Almond oil	LOX, MS, LAM, MSG
Avocado Oil	S, AM, MSG, PO (sorbitol)
Canola Oil	LOX, LS, LAM, F, PO
Corn Oil	MHOX, MS, AM
Olive Oil	LOX, HS, AM
Palm oil	LOX
Peanut Oil	M-HOX, MS, AM, MSG
Rice Bran Oil	VLS, LAM
Safflower Oil	LOX, LS
Sesame Oil	VHOX, MS, AM
Soybean Oil	VL-HOX, LS, MSG
Sunflower Oil	LOX, LS
Vegetable oil	LOX, Varies S

Walnut oil	M-HOX, M-HS, AM
	VINEGARS
Apple Cider Vinegar	VLOX, VHS, HAM, F, PO (sorbitol)
Balsamic vinegar	VLOX, HS, VHAM, HMSG, F
Cider vinegar	L-MOX, VHS, AM, F
Vinegar white/ red/wine	L-MOX, VHS, AM
Vinegar cider	L-MOX, VHS, AM, LF, PO (sorbitol)
Vinegar malt	L-MOX, AM

MEAT

Beef	LOX, LMSG
Beef, kidney	MOX, VHMSG
Beef liver	MOX, LAM, VHMSG
Corned beef	LOX
Lamb	LOX, LAM, LMSG
Pork	LOX, LAM, MMSG
Ham	LOX, HS, LAM, MSG
Bacon	LOX, H-VHAM, MMSG
Veal	LAM, LMSG

Chicken (no skin)	LOX, LMSG
Turkey (no skin)	LAM, HMSG
Rabbit	LAM
Lunch meat, seasoned	VHS, HAM, MSG
Meat canned	LOX, MS, LAM, MSG
Tripe	LAM, VHMSG
Organ meat not liver	MOX
Sausages	MOX, VHS, VHAM, MSG

SEAFOOD

Very fresh white fish	LOX, LS, LAM
Very fresh calamari	LS, LAM
Very fresh scallops	LOX, LS, LAM
Very fresh oysters	LOX, LS, LAM

Very fresh mussels	LOX, LS, LAM
Fresh crab	LOX, LS, LAM
Fresh Lobster	LOX, LS, LAM
Fresh salmon	LS, MAM
Fresh tuna	LS, MAM
Fresh sardines	MOX, LS, MAM
Very fresh prawns	LOX, LS
Fish roe	S, VHAM
Shellfish	LOX, LS
Shrimp paste	AM, MSG
Seaweed	HOX, HS, HAM, HMSG, F, PO (mannose)
Fish canned	HS, AM, MSG, PO (methanol/aspartame)
Anchovies	VHAM
Fish paste	LOX, VHMSG

MY FINAL WORDS

The research that I have done over the past 5 years and right up until now is what I can offer anyone with an intolerance that needs a change in their diet. The information may not be totally correct because most sites have different information on them depending on the issues they are talking about and I use the information that appears the same on at least two different sites.

I am aware that there are so many other foods that I haven't mentioned; however, many haven't been tested and are not listed. I have also learned a lot more about what is in foods and although I am not intending to write another cookbook in the near future, I still intend to keep up with my research.

I follow this diet chart and some of the foods I can tolerate; however, there are still a lot many more that I can't.

If I feel like trying something that I used to eat, I do and note the reaction that I have and how long it takes to come on.

I have learnt a new way to boil small red potatoes so that I am able to tolerate them more often in different ways; like in a potato salad. I can also tolerate a little tomato paste now, whereas before I could only use dried tomato skins as flavouring in different recipes.

I would again like to thank everybody who has contributed the information for me to use to write this book and I hope that by bringing all their information together, we are able to help you or someone you know to find a better diet and an easier way to live.

Please visit the web sites in the book if you wish to know more about one of the medical issues that I have mentioned as they explain them in more detail.

Have fun cooking and experiment with different recipes and ingredients that suit you and your family and you may get a wonderful surprise when you invent something new and tasty to eat without the issues.

www.ingramcontent.com/pod-product-compliance
Lightning Source LLC
Chambersburg PA
CBHW060511030426
42337CB00015B/1847

* 9 7 8 0 6 4 8 2 2 0 6 2 6 *